Put The Damn Cart Up

13 Steps to a Life Worth Living

Super Dave Quinn, CEcD

Super Dave Quinn, CEcD

First Printing, 2024

ISBN: 979-8-9917440-0-3

Disclaimer

Website: www.SuperDaveQuinn.com

Table of Contents

Prayer and Dedication

*"But if serving the LORD seems undesirable to you, then choose for yourselves this day whom you will serve, whether the gods your ancestors served beyond the Euphrates, or the gods of the Amorites, in whose land you are living. But as for me and my household, we will serve the LORD." ~ **Joshua 24.15 NIV***

Raised the son of a King James Bible-following, front-pew-sitting, John 3:16-adhering Southern Baptist mother, I was destined to become a believer in Christ. If the church doors were open, I was inside. That meant every Wednesday night and twice on Sunday. The rule around our house was simple: I could leave on Friday to hunt, camp, or spend the weekend doing whatever I wanted, but come ten o'clock on Sunday, I'd better be cleaned up and strolling through the doors of First Baptist Church of Como, Texas, or there would be hell to pay.

And while I recognize not everyone may have the same belief system as I do, it is my sincere prayer that you will come to know the God I know and worship. You'll notice I have begun each chapter of this book with scripture first, followed by worldly wisdom, and that's because I have given the world a chance and found it lacking. Offering both and with scripture first is my acknowledgment that it is only through the redemptive power of Christ that I am now writing these words for you. They're given by Him, for you, through me. I acknowledge this work as his and pray you are inspired to seek him.

To my wife, Kimbra, and my three beautiful children, Griffin, Presli, and Pierson:

Thank you for giving me the time to write this, for showing me grace, for encouraging me, and for believing in me, even when I did not believe in myself. I am blessed to have you in my life, and I know God gave me exactly what I needed when he gave me each of you. I pray every day that God gives me the strength and courage to become the husband and father you deserve.

To Lorie:

Thank you for pushing me to be better, for always believing in me, and for forcing me to move outside my comfort zone. Thank you for going on this journey with me and supporting me when things felt like they were not moving forward. I am blessed beyond belief to have you as a friend.

To Jane:

Thank you for insisting that I finish the book and share my story with others. I could not have done it without your help and inspiration. Your encouraging words helped me fight through procrastination.

Preface

Are You Ready to Leave Fear Behind?

"Peace, I leave with you; my peace I give to you. I do not give to you as the world gives. Do not let not your hearts be troubled and do not be afraid."

*~ **John 14:27 NIV***

"Our deepest fear is not that we are inadequate. Our deepest fear is that we are powerful beyond measure. It is our light, not our darkness that most frightens us. We ask ourselves, who am I to be brilliant, gorgeous, talented, fabulous? Actually, who are you not to be? You are a child of God. Your decision to play small does not serve the world. There is nothing enlightened about shrinking so that other people won't feel insecure around you. We are all meant to shine, as children do. We were born to make manifest the glory of God that is within us. It's not just in some of us; it's in everyone. And as we let our own light shine, we unconsciously give other people permission to do the same. As we are liberated from our own fear, our presence automatically liberates others." ~ ***Our Deepest Fear by Marianne Williamson, A Return to Love***

Neo sat staring at the small colored pills. One blue. One red. The red pill represented an uncertain future—it would free him from the enslaving control of the machine-generated dream world, allowing him to escape into the real world. But choosing this path meant living the "truth of reality," a harsher and more difficult journey.

On the other hand, the blue pill represented a beautiful prison—it would lead him back to ignorance, living in confined comfort without want or fear within the simulated reality of the Matrix.

Just like Neo in the 1999 film *The Matrix*, you have a choice to make. But know this: In either case, you are responsible for making the choice and must face the consequences that follow. No one can choose for you, and even not making a choice is actually making a choice. My father-in-law is famous among family and friends for saying, "Not to decide is to decide." So, the choice is simple: Yes or No.

Are you willing to choose a life of enlightenment and take responsibility for what comes next? If yes, continue turning the pages, and let us begin our journey together. If not, then thank you for reading this far, and I will see you in the funny papers.

Introduction

"But the fruit of the Spirit is love, joy, peace, patience, kindness, goodness, faithfulness, gentleness, self-control; against such things there is no law."
~ Galatians 5:22–23 NIV

"Obstacles don't have to stop you. If you run into a wall, don't turn around and give up. Figure out how to climb it, go through it, or work around it." ~
Michael Jordan

How a Costco Shopping Cart Changed My Life

It was going to be a great day. I remember the day because it was a beautiful Saturday morning in December, and I had gotten permission to go to Costco on a Saturday! Now, you may be asking why that's such a big deal, and I will tell you. I am only allowed to go to Costco when my wife, Kimbra, says I can go. And then it's only with a list because I have a terrible habit of coming home with random things in bulk that we don't need. Massive jars of peanut butter. A year's supply of Ziploc bags that we don't need. Enough beef jerky to feed an army, which we also don't need. I just can't help myself. I love to roam the aisles and find all the things I didn't even know we needed.

Saturdays at Costco are usually pretty chaotic, but I love them. I love the energy and all the little sample items you get to try. This particular Saturday was no different, except that it was busier than usual because of the approaching holiday. I knew it would be a packed parking lot, but I wasn't worried because I have this ability to manifest front-row parking space. Seriously, parking spots just appear. It drives my kids crazy, but it just happens because I believe that the universe is saving me a place, and nine times out of ten, I get a front-row parking spot.

As I pulled into the parking lot, the first aisle contained no empty parking spaces, and so I drove around to the next aisle. Sure enough, there was an open spot in the front. I always give a little nod to God at this point and say thank you.

 As I was pulling into my space, I noticed a shopping cart parked in the middle of my spot. Seriously? I was instantly frustrated. I got out, took a picture of the offending cart, and returned it to the cart corral. While I walked it back, I counted the steps it took to put it back. Thirteen. Thirteen steps were all it took to put away the cart. I finished parking my car, and as I walked into the store, I did what any red-blooded American would do when they have been offended. I posted the picture of the shopping cart to Facebook and with the following comment:

This drives me crazy. #13steps. #BeKindReturn

I put away my phone and went about my shopping. The problem, though, was my mood. It had changed. I was now angry and frustrated at the world for being lazy. This random person had ruined my morning and wholly destroyed what was going to be a great day. I completed my list and made my way out of Costco. I then loaded up my car and headed home.

Once at home, I put everything away and then took a few moments to scan Facebook. It was then I realized my shopping cart comment had blown up. People were agreeing and expressing their frustration, commenting things like "Burn them at the stake" and "I hate people who don't put their carts up." Others made excuses and said, "Maybe they were disabled," "Maybe they had babies and couldn't leave the car." Still, others felt convicted. You could tell that perhaps they had once not put their carts away. To try and clarify my comment, I decided to intervene and set everything straight. I responded, "If you are disabled, I'm not mad at you. I am not that kind of person, but let us be real; nine times out of ten times, it has nothing to do with ability. Because we are so busy and so worried about what we have got to get done, we are not paying attention to everything else."

With in days, people started texting me pictures of different shopping carts and would include the number of steps it took with a hashtag like "It's #43steps, Dave, not #13steps", "More than #13Steps in the pouring rain" (people would send me accompanying pictures of themselves drenched), and "In the middle of a thunderstorm, bro, I'm putting my basket up cause Dave says I have to."

Seeing those posts and realizing that others shared my experience was relieving at first. But as time went on, maybe a month or two later, I had an epiphany that shifted my mindset regarding that whole situation. Looking back, I realized that I was in a beautiful mood at the moment just before I saw the cart. Saturday morning at Costco, for me, is like going to Six Flags. It was an excellent feeling. But after the shopping cart incident, I was in a foul mood. I remember thinking how silly it was to allow an abandoned shopping cart to ruin my day. Not only that, but I subsequently sent out a wave of negativity via social media into the world that just kept rippling through my social circle. I thought of all these different emotions caused by a shopping cart and how I let a total stranger impact my day.

So I asked myself a question, "How could I have changed the outcome of that?"

The answer was simple. Had I simply taken the cart, put it away, and viewed it as my gift to the world, I could have forever changed the world. That is such a little thing, right? Most people think to change the world, they must lead some big protest, end world hunger, or solve climate change. They feel hopeless about impacting their world. And yet, every day, we can put away an abandoned shopping cart and change the world.

Most people, however, react as I did. They get angry and then post to the world that, "Hey, somebody should have done something or not have done something." That seems to be the world in which we live. Whenever someone else doesn't comply with our standards, we cry foul and post it on social media for all the world to see.

But think for a moment. How would the world have been different if I had just accepted the responsibility of putting up the cart? How would that have changed the world?

Let's first imagine that I had left the basket for the next person to find. Imagine a working mom with three little kids needing to get in and out of Costco for the Christmas party she is hosting that evening. Imagine her already stressed with the demands of Christmas time, working full time, and now having to herd three little ones through a busy Costco store on a Saturday. Having to fight an abandoned cart in the parking lot is the last thing she wants to do. But there it is, and she has to stop her car as she is pulling into a parking spot, get out of the car, and move the cart, all while leaving her babies strapped into their car seats, wondering what's going on.

She finally gets her car parked, but now she is frustrated and enters the store, yelling at the kids to stay close and to hurry up. She doesn't respond to the greeter. She bumps into another shopper as she tries to make the corner into the store and doesn't even say excuse me. She makes her rounds, giving off negative energy that can be felt by everyone around her. Unfortunately, no one knows the stress she is under, and they now walk away, feeling annoyed. She checks out and is short with the clerk, who is already feeling overwhelmed by the busy holiday shoppers. She makes her way out to the car, loads the kids up, and justifies not returning the cart because it was there when she pulled in. And so it goes, over and over again. Waves and waves of negative energy pulsing out into the universe.

Now, let's rewind and pretend I accepted the responsibility of putting the cart up. The spot is open, and it's a welcomed blessing to the mom. Just a little nod from God that he's looking out for her. She parks and helps the kids from the car. She strolls into the store, smiling at the greeter. She bumps into another customer and says, "Excuse me" and "I'm so sorry." They smile and shake it off. She works through her list, smiling as she goes and radiating positive energy that can be felt by everyone around her. She is patient with the kids as they reach and grab for things as they pass. As she makes her way to the check-out line, she greets the clerk with a smile and asks them how they are doing, thanking them for working so hard and for being so efficient. She heads out to the car and unloads the cart. After shutting her trunk, she starts to head toward the corral when another customer says he'll take the cart for her.

Now, those are two totally different realities, all because I took responsibility for a cart and returned it to the corral. Instead of putting negativity into the world, I put thankfulness and gratitude out there, forever changing the world in a small way. In my little piece of the world, simply putting away a shopping cart changes the world.

We all have these "shopping cart" moments in our lives—simple actions that, when we take responsibility for them, can transform someone's day for the better. Consider a common scenario at work: you notice someone didn't empty the K-cup after making coffee. Instead of feeling frustrated, take a moment to remedy the situation. It takes just a second to open the machine, remove the used K-cup, and toss it in the trash. By choosing to perform this small task, you not only prevent your own irritation but also make the environment more pleasant for everyone. Be a difference maker, and remember that even small actions, like tossing a K-cup, can have a significant impact.

We all have the choice to see a need and fill it. If you see something that bothers you, then it probably bothers someone else. Take the time to step up and change the world by taking care of it. This one small adjustment in mindset opens the door for so much beautiful change in our world.

The abandoned shopping cart I found at Costco changed my life because it led to the realization that I had the power to choose my mindset. And changing our mindset and taking action is how we change the world.

Seeing the abandoned shopping cart as an opportunity to change the world and being grateful in that moment for having that easy of a task to change the world is a completely different feeling than my initial reaction of frustration. This has impacted other areas of my life as well. Things that used to frustrate me I now see as opportunities to create change. I see them as easy exercises to make a difference in the world.

You do not have to lead global movements. You can start to make change in your neighborhood with a wave. God gives us little moments to create positive change in our world and to feel happiness, joy, and connectedness. We don't have to wait for other people. It all starts with you.

Step 1 - 100% Personal Responsibility

"For we must all appear before the judgment seat of Christ, so that each of us may receive what is due us for the things done while in the body, whether good or bad." ~2 Corinthians 5:10 NIV

"The buck stops here." ~Unknown, popularized by President Harry S. Truman

Early in my marriage, I joined a men's church choir group that held practice on Wednesday evenings and would sing on Sunday. While waiting for everyone to arrive, I started a conversation with an older gentleman in the choir. Being a newlywed and needing some advice, I began telling the story about Kimbra and her habit of not replacing the toilet paper roll when it ran out. She would get a new one out, but she would not put it on. She just set it on the holder. It really frustrated me. My perspective was that it takes three seconds to put it on. Just put it on.

The older gentleman interjected and asked, "How long does it take to put it on?" To which I replied, "Three seconds, I timed it."

He then asked, "How often does this happen?" "Two or three times a month," I replied. He then said, "Let us say it is once a week for the entire month, so you spent twelve seconds doing something for your wife. Is your wife worth twelve seconds of your time?"

I had never really thought about it that way. His words had reframed that whole situation. It is silly now to think about it, but that little exchange has saved me years of frustration. It was one of the greatest pieces of marriage advice I ever received.

To reframe it, you can ask, "Is it worth fixing, or is it something that you can invest time wisely into making the relationship or the situation better?"

While it is tempting to blame others for our circumstances, accepting 100% responsibility for our actions is the beginning of peak performance. You are responsible for your actions—all of them. You are responsible for your thoughts and actions, whether deliberate or unintentional. You will make mistakes, but when you do, learn to take responsibility and make it right.

You are where you are because of who you are. Everything that exists in your life exists because of you, because of your behavior, words and actions, and reactions. Yes, there will be situations and times when people will do or say/do not do or say the things that you want, and you are going to feel entitled to blame them. But understand that when we blame others, we are literally giving power for negative feelings to take over.

Taking responsibility allows you the ability to choose how to respond to a challenge and gives you the power to control a situation positively. Most of all, taking 100% ownership and responsibility changes your energy and puts you in a calmer state of mind. Taking 100% ownership of everything in your domain, including the outcome and everything that it impacts, is the most fundamental building block of a life worth living.

The Buck Stops Here!

President Harry S. Truman's famous motto, "the buck stops here"—which he had displayed on a sign he kept on his Oval Office desk—is derived from poker game play, "passing the buck." Today, it has come to mean "passing blame" or absolving oneself of responsibility or concern by denying authority or jurisdiction over a given matter. In his January 1953 farewell address to the American people, President Truman referred to this concept very specifically in asserting that "The President—whoever he is—has to decide. He cannot pass the buck to anyone. No one can do the deciding for him. That is his job."

In his book, *The Travelers Gift*, Andy Andrews uses this phrase as a simple way to frame the concept that to achieve personal success, you must accept personal responsibility for your past. You must understand that the beginning of wisdom is to accept responsibility for your own problems and that by accepting responsibility for your past, you set yourself free to move into a bigger, brighter future of your own choosing.

When you accept that you control your thoughts and your emotions, you can begin to change where you are—mentally, physically, spiritually, emotionally, and financially. You can change all of these by changing the way you think. Simply put, The Buck Stops Here.

How to Take 100% Personal Responsibility

- **Choose your thoughts:** You have been created to live a life of freedom, health, and wealth. If your life doesn't reflect that, your thoughts might be the barrier. Thoughts are powerful—they can create happiness and wealth or bring about sickness and poverty. If your reality doesn't match your dreams, it's time to shift your mindset.

Remember, you alone control your thoughts. No one can put a thought in your head without your permission. Learn to master and guard your thoughts. Choose them wisely.

- **Accept Responsibility:** When things go wrong, resist the urge to make excuses or blame others. Instead, take full responsibility. By doing so, you regain control and can learn from the situation to create future success. Pointing fingers makes you a bystander in your own life. Owning your part, however small, forces you to confront your weaknesses and grow from them. Next time you feel like blaming, pause, breathe, and reflect on your role in the situation. Accept reality, take ownership, and move forward.

- **Power of Choice**: Saying "I don't have a choice" is a passive trap. You always have a choice, even if it's by default. Acknowledge your options to develop a sense of personal responsibility.

Use intentional language to build ownership of your decisions:

"I choose to scroll through Facebook instead of playing with my kids."

"I choose not to go to the gym tonight."

"I choose to eat comfort food over nourishing food."

"I choose to watch TV instead of reading."

This practice helps you recognize when you're making excuses and encourages conscious decision-making.

- **Become Accountable**: Create a framework of accountability in your life. Share your goals with people who will hold you accountable. This support system makes you more likely to take ownership of your actions and provides additional support when things get tough, preventing you from slipping back into unproductive habits.

- **Get Comfortable With Discomfort**: Sorry, no way else to say it. Living a fulfilling life means stepping outside your comfort zone. Blaming external forces keeps you safe but stagnant. Growth requires discomfort. Embrace the challenge and be willing to push your boundaries for a life worth living.

- **Stop Complaining**: Complaining is a form of playing the victim. It indicates a lack of focus and control. Instead of complaining, ask yourself, "What can I do to improve this situation?" Taking proactive steps turns negative energy into positive action.

- **Stop Taking Everything So Personally**: Not everything is about you. Taking disagreements personally is not a sign of ownership. You can't control others' actions, only your response. When faced with a disagreement, ask yourself if it's about the issue or if you're making it personal. Asking questions instead of making assumptions is liberating.

I promise that taking responsibility for your thoughts, actions, and life will be challenging. It requires learning and growing from your mistakes. But it will also allow you to create a fulfilling, meaningful life. You have the freedom to choose. Choose wisely.

Step 2 - Gratitude

"Let the message of Christ dwell among you richly as you teach and admonish one another with all wisdom through psalms, hymns, and songs from the Spirit, singing to God with Gratitude in your hearts." **~Colossians 3:16**

"Of all the attitudes a person can acquire, the attitude of gratitude is the most important and by far the most life changing." **~Zig Ziglar**

I remember learning this lesson on U.S. Highway 87 just outside of San Angelo, Texas, while moving my family for a new job. Kimbra and I were driving the moving vans from our home in Levelland down to Bastrop, Texas. As we passed the last gas station on our way out of San Angelo, I noticed we had a little over a quarter of a tank of gas. Thinking it would be enough to get us to the next town and pushing to get to Bastrop as early as possible, I made the decision to drive on. About fifteen miles out, the truck started to sputter and then ran out of fuel. Seeing the gauge still showed 1/4 of a tank, I was fuming. Pun intended.

I called U-Haul, and they knew right away which truck I was driving. They said it was a common occurrence, and someone should have told me at the time of renting. So, as I sat on the side of the road in the hot Texas heat, I contemplated posting about the whole ordeal on social media. I was feeling angry and upset, having been delayed by a faulty fuel gauge that was a known issue. Then I realized something profound.

While it was an inconvenience, it was not as bad as what my friends had endured in Bastrop, Texas, just six weeks earlier. They had lost everything in the 2011 Bastrop County Complex fire. Out of four couples, three had lost everything they owned. How could I possibly be upset? I was sitting there in perfect health, looking at all my worldly possessions. Safe and sound inside the moving truck. Instantly, the anger drained from me. I said a quick prayer to thank God for the blessing and the reminder.

What is gratitude?

A quick Google search for the definition of gratitude will give you this definition: Gratitude - the quality of being thankful; readiness to show appreciation for and to return kindness. It comes from the Latin word "gratus," which means "thankful, pleasing." In general terms, Gratitude is the appreciation of what is valuable to you.

Being thankful for what you have or have worked toward and showing this appreciation to others.

Research shows that practicing gratitude is beneficial to our emotional wellness, and these benefits also carry over into other aspects of wellness. Gratitude increases our happiness and makes us healthier. Being grateful elicits the relaxation response, which causes the brain to release chemicals that slow down our muscles and organs and increase blood flow to the brain. Practicing gratitude also helps you sleep better and is beneficial to your body (physical wellness).

Gratitude strengthens relationships, makes you a better friend to others (social wellness), and boosts overall wellbeing. In addition to getting rid of negativity and improvement of moods, recent studies show that feeling and expressing gratitude can also improve one's physical health. A professor of family medicine and public health at the University of California San Diego School of Medicine, Paul Mills, conducted studies that explained the role of gratitude on heart health. Among other things, he found that people who kept a gratitude journal had reduced levels of inflammation and improved heart rhythm.

How to Develop an Attitude of Gratitude

Developing an attitude of gratitude takes practice, just like anything else. Sometimes, it may seem impossible to be grateful, but making a daily habit of recognizing the blessings around you is crucial for your mental health, just as physical activity is crucial for your physical health. Focus on specific situations, both big and small, that you can be thankful for. This practice helps you take control of your mind.

It's essential to do this every single day, not just by saying "thank you," but by truly stepping into those moments and feeling the gratitude and aliveness that comes with being appreciative.

Tony Robbins calls gratitude the antidote to life's challenges. For instance, you can't be angry and grateful at the same time, nor can you be fearful and grateful simultaneously. Gratitude is a solution to both anger and fear.

Even the simple act of waking up should create gratitude, considering that many people don't wake up each day. Tomorrow is promised to no one, and recognizing each new day as a blessing helps keep things in perspective. Every day won't be perfect, but focusing on what we are grateful for can wash away feelings of anger, frustration, and negativity.

Having an attitude of gratitude means living with a constant appreciation for everything you have. Your state of mind and attitude are crucial to your overall health, often more than people realize. Gratitude is a powerful force that keeps our minds healthy. Approaching any situation with gratitude can alleviate suffering and provide a more objective and rational perspective.

When we forget to practice gratitude, we can easily spiral into negative emotions such as depression, regret, guilt, sorrow, anger, and fear. Neglecting gratitude opens the door to unhealthy behaviors. Activities like gossiping, dishonesty, and spending excessive time on social media or watching mindless television become unappealing to someone who lives in a state of gratitude.

Developing an attitude of gratitude and being thankful for everything you have will lead to contentment, resulting in peace, happiness, and extreme joy. It will also help you maintain a positive outlook on life, especially in times of trouble. Moreover, gratitude can provide you with insight and allow you to see just how much you have to be grateful for.

"How," you ask, "can I develop an attitude of gratitude? What are the things I can do and steps I can take?" I'm so glad you asked.

Here are some tips on developing an attitude of gratitude, along with the exercises I most often use to engage in a practice of gratitude.

- **Develop a Habit of Saying "Thank You"**: Gratitude is one of the best gifts you can give someone. A simple "thank you" can make a person feel appreciated. Imagine a waiter having a tough day serving you at a restaurant. You might think you don't need to say "thank you" because you paid for your meal. But saying "thank you" can bring a smile to their face and make their day better. You might not realize it, but you've brightened someone's day. Make saying "thank you" a habit.

- **Show Gratitude with Small Gifts**: It is absolutely true that "It's the thought that counts" when it comes to the best gifts. Showing gratitude through gift-giving doesn't have to be expensive. The smallest things, like a little bar of chocolate, a sticky note, a gift card, or a greeting card, can go a long way. Gifts are always appropriate to recognize something specific someone has done for you. They're also great to give when you see someone who may need a little encouragement, just to show you appreciate what they bring to life.

- **Keep a Gratitude Journal**: Keep a journal where you can express your gratitude. Each day, jot down specifically what you are thankful for and watch how your gratitude grows over time. You may start with a small list, but soon you'll discover countless things to be grateful for.

- **Meditate:** This is helpful to do daily, even for just five minutes. It is especially helpful when negativity sets in, and you may not feel appreciative or grateful for anything. If you're unfamiliar with meditation, it is more straightforward than it may sound and becomes even easier with practice. To meditate on a spirit of thankfulness, find a quiet space, breathe deeply and slowly, and relax your muscles as you clear your mind of all present thoughts. After a minute or two, shift your mind to think only about who and what you are thankful for. Once you bring these thoughts to mind, you will feel a shift from negativity to positivity. If you've never tried meditation and you want to learn more beyond my simple explanation, there are many resources and even free apps available if you prefer a guided approach.

- **Show Gratitude Even in Difficult Situations:** Gratitude isn't just for the good times—it's especially powerful in difficult moments. In challenging situations, the positives often stand out more when you actively look for them. This helps you focus on what you can be thankful for, even when things seem tough. Reflect on your current struggles and identify what's going right. Look back at past challenges and consider the valuable lessons you learned. And always remember—difficult times don't last forever.

- **Express Your Gratitude Fully**: This applies to saying "thank you" and gift-giving, but it also means expressing your gratitude in all you say and do. It is not enough to just keep your gratitude to yourself in a journal. Passing it along through notes and gifts or even speaking it when appropriate amplifies the feeling. Show your feelings of gratitude by how you interact with people each day. That means treating others with respect, genuine interest, and generosity of spirit. William Ward once said, "Feeling gratitude and not expressing it is like wrapping a present and not giving it."

- **Spending Time With Your Loved Ones**: Your loved ones are probably high on your list of what you're grateful for, and spending time with them reinforces that feeling. In general, it helps you grow closer and strengthens those relationships, and every moment spent is an opportunity to show your gratitude for them. It also helps when you're struggling with negativity and may not feel so grateful, as their presence should quickly remind you to shift those thoughts.

- **Celebrate the Little Things:** Many people are so focused on achieving the big things and becoming successful that they forget to put things into perspective and realize just how lucky they already are. If you only celebrate the big things and the wins that bring highs, you will tend to lose sight of the little things that bring the most joy and gratitude. Take the time each day to reflect on all the small moments when you have achieved something—even the smallest moments that stood out for you. These things are just as worthy of your gratitude journal as any other.

- **Surround Yourself with Positive People**: Energy is contagious. If you surround yourself with negative people, their outlook can rub off on you. Conversely, positive people can uplift and motivate you. Surround yourself with positive influences to help you grow and reach your goals.

Over the years, I have learned a couple of ways to help me in building my own attitude of gratitude. Here are two exercises I would like to share with you that can help you on your path to a life of gratitude.

Give Me 5:

First thing in the morning, right after you wake up, take those first precious minutes to think about five people in your life for whom you are grateful. Picture each one of them individually. Think about the many ways the individual has touched your life. Picture looking them in the eye, noticing the color of their eyes, and saying thank you. Then, picture them laughing and being full of joy and happiness, and send them your gratitude once again. This will help you begin the day focused on what's most important to you. This also helps you when you find yourself in a low self-esteem moment. You can simply close your eyes and repeat this process, remembering the people who love you and care for you.

This exercise reminds you just how rich you are in life and allows you to pull out of a depressed mode. To help you start this habit, place a sticky note on your bathroom mirror. When you walk into the bathroom for the first time and see it on the mirror, I'm giving you permission to get back in bed and do this exercise.

Write Two and Call in Me the Morning:

Each day, while you are drinking your morning coffee or tea, handwrite at least two thank-you notes. That's it.

Now, some days, it may need to be more, but the idea is to write two of them before you jump into the business of your day. Doing this forces you to become more aware of the people in your daily life that help you. At first, you will write some pretty obvious thank-you notes. You'll write one to a colleague who helps you often. You may write to a vendor who did something particularly helpful for you. But at some point, it may get a little tougher to identify just who might deserve a thank-you note from you. This is where the magic starts to happen.

Your subconscious mind, knowing that it has a task to write thank-you notes, will begin to take notice of moments that deserve your gratitude. The barista who smiled so brightly at you that it lifted your morning. Or maybe the security guard in the lobby who always sends you a smile and a nod as you stroll by. Write a thank-you note to the person who takes in your dry cleaning and notice how they greet you the next time you drop off your clothes. If you have never written a handwritten thank-you note to your spouse or to your child, I challenge you to do so and watch how they light up when they receive the note.

Life is filled with these little moments every day, and we often take them for granted. So go ahead and write two in the morning and call me. Seriously . . . I can't wait to hear how it goes.

Starting each day with a bit of gratitude allows the rest of life to take care of itself. It doesn't mean things will not go wrong. Or that everything is rosy, but it does mean that when things do go wrong, you will be in a better mental space to tackle the challenges. I promise investing in building an Attitude of Gratitude will have a profound impact on your emotional wellbeing.

Step 3 - Define Your Success

"In everything he did he had great success, because the LORD was with him."
~1 Samuel 18:14 NIV

'Success is doing what you love, providing for your family while doing it, and being true to yourself." **~Drew Myers, Podcast host and author**

Kimbra and I once met with a financial planner and decided to move our various retirement accounts under his care. Organizing our retirement plan was something we knew needed to be done, but it always seemed like a hassle to gather up all the various accounts, so we kept putting it off.

Until now. The actual moving of accounts wasn't that hard. Most of our accounts had online access, and we were able to look everything up and provide our planner with the necessary information. Interestingly enough, the hardest part of the whole process was a questionnaire he sent us. We sat down at the table, full of excitement to map out our future. That excitement quickly turned into something very different when we realized we didn't know what we wanted our future to look like. We also discovered that my vision of the future was very different from Kimbra's. The exercise encouraged us to dream big. So, while I was envisioning private air travel and month-long vacations in far-off lands, Kimbra was much more practical, thinking about paying for our grandkids' college or buying their first cars upon graduation.

As we continued with the exercise, it only got more challenging. Eventually, we decided to shelve the whole activity until a later date. As of this writing, we are still waiting for that "someday" to finish the exercise.

"You can get what you want, but first, you have to know what you want." ~ Super Dave Quinn, CEcD

This statement has come out of my mouth more often than I can count. I have three beautiful children, and it's crazy how hard it is for them to figure out what they want. Whether it's choosing which candy to get from the convenience store on a long road trip or picking which college to attend, these decisions can be debilitating because they aren't sure of what they really want. Salty or sweet? A long way from home or close enough to swing by for dinner when the pantry is empty?

If I'm being honest, it's not all that surprising. I've been married to their mother for more than 25 years, and I still have trouble figuring out what that beautiful redhead wants.

There is one thing I know Kimbra wants: to travel. We love to travel, and many of our adventures include road trips. Once the car is loaded and we're all buckled in, the first step is to type our desired destination into Google. That's it. Even if we've never been there before, we simply put in the destination, and Google will take us there. It might involve a few flights, boat rides, donkey rides, and some walking, but knowing the destination helps us figure out how to get there.

The great thing about knowing your destination is that you also know when you're getting off course. It happens. Just like on road trips, unexpected things pop up, and you have to take a detour. But a simple recalculation can get you back on track. Without a destination, you just roam from place to place, wasting precious time and energy. Unless, of course, your definition of success is to be a nomad and roam from place to place with no plan.

It's essential to treat your mind the same way. As humans, we need to understand where we are heading, how long or how much work it will take, and what the reward will be once we get there.

Part of building resilience in our lives is developing the habit of framing any project by clearly defining these key elements:

Destination (Goal): What is the end result you want to achieve?

Plan (Steps): What steps are needed to get there?

Timeframe: How long will it take?

Reward: What will be the reward once you reach your goal?

Surprises will come up, but if you know your destination is worthwhile, you can better handle challenges as they arise.

It's not complicated when you think about it. What do you want? That's it. Simply begin with the end in mind. Create a plan and then execute the plan.

What if I told you that it is very possible to be successful? The successful life worth living is within your reach, and all you need to do is take certain steps to get it.

To be truthful, attaining success and reaching your goals is not as complicated as it sounds. However, it requires hard work and dedication. Here are some simple steps to follow to become successful, however you choose to define it.

How to Define and Map Your Success

- **Define what Success Means to You**: Before you can attain the life you are dreaming about, the life worth living, you must know what kind of life you want. What are you working toward? What does success mean to you? For some, it might mean a flexible job that allows them to travel and work from anywhere in the world. For others, it might mean buying a beautiful house with a beautiful view. Do some deep thinking. What does success mean to you, and what kind of life would you like to live? Many of us already had some idea years ago about what life would look like right now. Are you living that? Is that still what you want? If not, what is? Accept that your definition of success can change over time, and it probably already has.

- **Create Your Vision:** Start by envisioning your future. Ask yourself if your vision has changed over time. Is your vision long-term or short-term? Imagine how you will feel once your vision becomes a reality. Write it down in detail, picturing your life in the next year, five years, ten years. Describe everything, from the smells and places to the people around you and your reactions to your success.

- **Set Goals for Your Vision:** While the vision is a clear image of your future, goals are specific targets that move

31

you toward that vision. Set specific, measurable goals to stay focused and on track. Break down your ultimate goals into smaller, more manageable steps. For example, if your goal is to buy a luxury house, determine how much you need to earn per month or quarter to make that a reality. Be flexible and adjust your goals as needed.

- **Align Your Vision with Your Business Goals:** Ensure your business goals align with your personal goals. Your work and personal life are intertwined, so compare the two visions and make adjustments if they don't align. This harmony will help you achieve success in both areas.

- **Track Your Successes**: Keep a journal to document your daily accomplishments, no matter how small. Over time, you'll see your progress and identify areas for improvement. This practice will motivate you and help you stay on track.

- **Celebrate Every Success:** Celebrate every success, big or small. Each achievement is a step toward your ultimate goal. Recognizing these moments keeps you motivated and creates momentum. Share your celebrations with others to spread positivity.

- **Get Educated:** Educate yourself thoroughly before diving into any new endeavor. Understanding the mechanics of your chosen field will prevent you from making costly mistakes and giving up prematurely. Knowledge is a powerful tool for success.

- **Keep Learning:** Make a lifelong commitment to learning. Stay updated, read books, and expand your knowledge in every possible way. Continuous learning opens your mind to new opportunities and increases your intellectual capacity.

- **Network:** Networking is crucial for success. Connect with people, seek mentors, and get involved in your community. Jim Rohn said, "You are the average of the five people you spend the most time with." Surround yourself with positive influences and potential opportunities.

- **Be Consistent:** Discipline and consistency are key to success. Once you know what you want and how to achieve it, work tirelessly toward your goals. Be prepared to make sacrifices and invest a lot of time and effort. Consistency is essential for overcoming challenges and achieving success.

Remember, achieving success isn't easy. Along the way, you will encounter roadblocks and face moments of frustration, exhaustion, and setbacks. But trust in your strength and determination. You don't need to see the entire path right now. Focus on taking the next best step. Each step forward will reveal the next one, guiding you closer to your goals. Stay committed to doing your best for yourself and your loved ones. Trust in yourself and keep moving forward, one step at a time.

Step 4 - Find Your Purpose

*"The one who plants and the one who waters have one purpose, and they will each rewarded according to their own labor." ~**1 Corinthians 3:8 NIV***

*"He who has a why to live can bear almost any how." ~ **Viktor Frankl***

As mentioned, we love to travel, and many of our trips are road trips with our kids. To ensure a pleasant journey, Kimbra and I have learned that we need to do a few basic things before we ever leave the driveway. First, we share our destination with our kids. Then, we explain how long it will take to get there, and finally, we discuss what we plan to do once we arrive.

This might seem like a simple example, but for anyone with kids, it makes perfect sense. It can be incredibly frustrating to get everyone moving in the same direction without first clearly defining the destination, the time and effort required, and the expected outcome.

This lesson, learned from my personal life, has been invaluable in my professional life as well. Clearly communicating your purpose and plan to others helps align everyone's efforts and expectations. When people understand the destination, the journey, and the rewards, they are more likely to be motivated and cooperative.

Sharing your purpose is essential for achieving success, both in personal and professional contexts. It builds trust, fosters collaboration, and ensures that everyone is working toward the same goal. This is why it's so important to spend time identifying your purpose—so you can clearly and effectively share it with others.

The Importance of Meaning and Purpose

At some point in your life, you may have asked yourself these questions: "What should I do with my life?" "What is my passion?" and "What is my purpose?" You might be doing something now that you enjoy, but with deeper exploration, you may discover that you are passionate about something entirely different.

Psychologists have studied goals and found that meaningful long-term ones tend to develop throughout our lives. Goals embedded in a sense of purpose are the ones that can potentially change the lives of others, like starting an organization, researching a cure for a disease, or teaching.

A sense of purpose seems to have evolved in humans to help us accomplish big things. This is why purpose is associated with both physical and mental health. It's adaptive in an evolutionary sense— it's a survival mechanism for humans.

Most people measure success by the wealth they accumulate, the power they gain, or the status they achieve. Yet, even when they reach success beyond their wildest dreams, they often feel empty inside, as if something is missing. That missing element is PURPOSE.

Finding your purpose is about finding your "WHY."

Whether you are an entrepreneur, an employee, a homemaker, a team leader, a team member, or just someone seeking clarity for your next move, your WHY is the constant that will guide you toward fulfillment.

WHY can be defined as the purpose, the belief, the cause, or the force that drives you. WHY does your career exist? WHY did you get out of bed this morning? And WHY should you care?

Your WHY is what makes you different from everyone else. It is your purpose, and it inspires you to take action. Not only does it inspire you, but it also inspires others.

The Centers for Disease Control and Prevention (CDC) acknowledge that a sense of purpose is an essential component of mental health. People with good mental health have qualities like "self-acceptance, openness to new experiences, optimism, hopefulness, purpose in life, control of one's environment, spirituality, self-direction, and positive relationships" (Mental Health Basics, 2013).

Some of you may be familiar with the book *Man's Search for Meaning*, written by psychiatrist Viktor Frankl. If you haven't read it, I highly recommend it. It's not only a story about one man's experience inside a Nazi concentration camp during World War II but also about Frankl's theories on what helped some survive while many others perished.

Frankl believed that our thoughts and beliefs about a situation are things we can always choose, regardless of our circumstances. He believed that finding meaning could be the difference between living or dying in the camp. In his book, he says, "He who knows the 'why' for his existence can bear almost any 'how.'"

Finding and holding on to meaning and purpose can help us overcome even the most difficult situations and challenges. Understanding your purpose helps make suffering more bearable.

By understanding what your one thing is, you can build a life you desire and find joy and fulfillment in—this is because you can see how the work you do relates to your purpose.

I have realized that each person is born with a unique life purpose. The most important action a successful person can take is to identify, acknowledge, and honor this purpose. You must take the time to understand what you are here to do and then pursue that realization with passion and enthusiasm.

Purpose is a conscious, intentional goal that is sought after and pursued for a desired effect. Examples of such purposes include getting a degree, developing a career, engaging in a hobby, building a relationship, getting married, or raising children. These goals are indeed purposes because they promote a person's life and make it meaningful.

For some of us, we have already realized our purpose and passion in life, and it is evident and clear to us. We are all born with a set of talents, and through consistent practice, we develop those talents into skills.

You may be asking yourself, "Can a person have more than one purpose?" The answer is absolutely! Life is multifaceted, and individuals often find meaning in various aspects of their lives. A person might have a professional purpose in their career, a personal purpose in their family life, and a community purpose in volunteer work. Having multiple purposes can enrich a person's life, providing diverse sources of fulfillment and motivation. As we grow and our circumstances change, our purposes can evolve and expand, contributing to a richer, more satisfying life.

In summary, the conscious, intentional goals you pursue—be it in education, career, relationships, or personal development—are all valid purposes. Embracing multiple purposes allows for a well-rounded and meaningful life.

How to Find Your Purpose and Know Your WHY

- **Explore Things You Love to Do**: Everyone is born with a deep and meaningful purpose to discover. Your purpose isn't something you have to create; it already exists within you. Uncover your purpose by asking yourself, "What do I love doing?" and "What comes naturally to me?" While it may take time and effort to identify your talent, when you do find it, it should feel natural and fulfilling, like a passion for teaching, writing, mentoring, helping others through volunteering, or cooking.

- **Follow Your Inner Guidance:** We all have an inner guidance system that helps us distinguish right from wrong and guides us on the right path. This inner guidance works like a GPS, directing us from our current location to our desired destination. Listen to your heart and let it guide you toward your goals and vision.

- **Be Clear About Your Life Purpose:** Clarity of purpose is essential for living a fulfilling life. When you are clear about your purpose and keep your mind focused on it, you can achieve it more easily. The things that bring you the greatest joy and passion are often aligned with your purpose.

- **Create a Life Purpose Statement:** To create a life purpose statement, start by reflecting on what truly matters to you. Consider the activities and causes that bring you joy and fulfillment. Think about the moments when you felt most alive and engaged, and identify the common themes in those experiences. Ask yourself questions like, "What impact do I want to have on the world?" and "What do I want to be remembered for?" Write down your thoughts, focusing on the core values and passions that drive you. Aim for a concise and inspiring statement that encapsulates your vision for your life.

For example, "My purpose is to inspire others to take ownership of their lives to positively impact the world by sharing their God-given talents and abilities." This statement should serve as a guiding light, helping you stay focused on your goals and aligned with your true self.

- **Listen to Feedback**: Sometimes, it's hard to recognize your passions on your own. Others may see your passions and strengths more clearly. Ask three people what they associate with you or what comes to mind when they think of you. Take note of compliments and observations, and look for patterns that point to your purpose.

- **Consider Things That Deeply Concern You:** Your purpose may be connected to issues that deeply upset you. What injustices or problems in the world make you want to take action? Whether it's animal welfare, women's rights, homelessness, or substance abuse, finding what bothers you can lead you to your passion.

Reflect on what your perfect life looks like. What kind of job would you have? Where would you live? By consistently asking these questions, you can trigger your subconscious mind to guide you toward your ideal life. If you're not feeling happy or fulfilled, it's time to reevaluate your life's purpose. It's never too late to start living the life you want—a meaningful and joyful life. Find your purpose and take action to create the life you desire.

Finding Your Purpose Exercise

Here is a little exercise to help you develop a simple but powerful statement of your life purpose. This is a compelling statement to help guide and direct your behavior moving forward. Take some time now to complete the following exercise.

First, list two of your unique personal qualities, such as *enthusiasm* and *creativity*.

1. _____

2. _____

Next, list one or two ways you enjoy expressing those qualities when interacting with others, such as to *support* and *inspire*.

1. _____

2. _____

Now, assume the world is perfect right now. What does this world look like? How is everyone interacting with everyone else? What does it feel like? Write your answer as a statement, in the present tense, describing the ultimate condition, the perfect world as you see it and feel it. Remember, a perfect world is a fun place to be.

Example: Everyone is freely expressing their own unique talents. Everyone is working in harmony. Everyone is expressing love.

_____

_____

_____

_____

Finally, combine the three prior subdivisions of this paragraph into a single statement.

Example: My purpose is to use my creativity and enthusiasm to support and inspire others to freely express their talents in a harmonious and loving way.

_____

_____

_____

_____

Step 5 - Choose Your Thoughts

"We demolish arguments and every pretension that sets itself up against the knowledge of God, and we take captive every thought to make it obedient to Christ." ~2 Corinthians 10:5 NIV

"Thoughts create our feelings and feelings drive our actions and actions create our results" ~Super Dave Quinn, CEcD

My wife Kimbra used to work at South Plains College, a community college in Levelland, Texas. Because it was a small West Texas college, the demographics were primarily first-generation college students, many of whom were Hispanic. It was fascinating to see how these first-generation Hispanic students, especially the women, often chose not to use their Spanish language skills. They didn't want others to know they were Hispanic and could speak Spanish, seeing it as a liability.

Kimbra made a significant impact by helping them realize that being bilingual was actually an incredible asset. She taught them the value of speaking two languages and helped them change their thoughts about their abilities. She empathized with their feelings and understood why they held that belief, but she was able to open their eyes to a new reality and value.

Your mind is the most powerful tool you can use to create your future. However, like an undisciplined 3-year-old, if left unchecked, it can lead to some destructive behaviors. Have you ever considered what you are thinking about? How often do you stop and question why you are having certain thoughts? Have you ever had a thought that made you laugh, become angry, or feel sad? It happens to me all the time. Sometimes I wish we had an on/off button for our thoughts or a select and delete button.

Let me paint a scenario: Our minds are very similar to a radio. You can choose which station to listen to, switching between music genres like rock, folk, jazz, oldies, or any other you prefer. If you don't want to listen, you can turn off the radio. The part everyone wishes for is the ability to turn off thoughts as easily as a radio. While deep breathing and meditation are the closest things to turning off our thoughts, it's not exactly easy.

Thoughts have power. Great, creative power. If you can train your mind to work for you and not against you, you will achieve so much more. James Allen once said, "You are today where your thoughts have brought you; you will be tomorrow where your thoughts take you." Sometimes, your thoughts might come rushing in all at once, both the positive and negative ones. It is possible to filter your thoughts and select the ones you want to focus on.

How to Begin Filtering Your Thoughts

- **Start with Awareness:** Begin by simply noticing your thoughts. Pay attention to the patterns and themes that run through your mind. This awareness is the first step to understanding and filtering your thoughts.

- **Practice Mindfulness:** Spend a few minutes each day practicing mindfulness. Focus on your breathing and observe your thoughts without judgment. This practice helps you become more present and less reactive to negative thoughts.

- **Challenge Negative Thoughts:** When a negative thought arises, question its validity. Ask yourself, "Is this thought true?" "Is it helpful?" Replace negative thoughts with positive affirmations or more balanced perspectives.

- **Keep a Thought Journal:** Write down your thoughts daily. This helps you track patterns and identify recurring negative thoughts. Over time, you'll see which thoughts need more attention and filtering.

- **Surround Yourself with Positivity:** Fill your environment with positive influences. Read inspiring books, listen to uplifting music, and spend time with supportive people. Positive surroundings can help shift your mindset and filter out negativity.

- **Set Intentions:** Start your day with clear intentions. Decide how you want to feel and what you want to focus on. Setting intentions helps guide your thoughts in a positive direction.

- **Use Visualization:** Visualize your ideal day or a specific goal. Picture yourself succeeding and feeling happy. Visualization can help rewire your brain to focus on positive outcomes.

- **Practice Gratitude:** Each day, write down three things you are grateful for. Focusing on gratitude shifts your mind away from negative thoughts and helps you appreciate the positive aspects of your life.

- **Limit Negative Inputs:** Be mindful of the media you consume. Limit exposure to negative news, social media, or anything that brings you down. Choose content that inspires and uplifts you.

- **Seek Professional Help if Needed:** If you find it challenging to manage your thoughts, don't hesitate to seek help from a therapist or coach. They can provide tools and techniques to help you filter your thoughts more effectively.

- Remember, filtering your thoughts is a practice. It takes time and patience, but with consistent effort, you can train your mind to focus on the positive and let go of the negative.

Step 6 - Focus on What Matters

"Let your eyes look straight ahead; fix your gaze directly before you."
~**Proverbs 4:25 NIV**

"Energy flows where attention goes." ~ ***Tony Robbins***

When I was ready to learn to drive, my dad took up the responsibility. One night, we happened to be driving at night on a dark highway in the piney woods of Northeast Texas. As we were driving, a car made the corner and began heading straight toward us. My Dad quickly grabbed the wheel and veered us to the right. You see, it was not the other car that was coming toward us. It was me heading toward them. I had locked in on their headlights and unconsciously steered our car toward where I was staring.

That was a valuable lesson. My dad explained that if I watched the white line on the right while glancing to my left, I could avoid drifting into the oncoming lane of traffic. This lesson has stuck with me ever since and served me in more than just nighttime driving. You see, whether you are on the golf course staring at a water hazard or sitting at your desk envisioning what might go wrong with your event, that same invisible force that pulled me into oncoming traffic causes you to direct your path toward what you are focusing on.

It is okay to acknowledge the hazards or the risks that lie ahead, but keep your focus on the desired outcome, and you will be much more successful. So now you ask, "Yeah, but how do I focus on what matters?"

Have you ever had trouble finding something in the garage or basement, but the only light you had was the fluorescent light in the center of the room? It can be a frustrating and infuriating experience.

Most days, that single defused light is perfectly fine. You are merely passing through the space, and you do not need much energy to get you safely across the garage. But when you are in desperate need of a small nut, washer, or thingamabob to complete a task, and it lies in the dark recesses of your junk shelf, the soft glow from the glass tubes just will not do. No, you need a beam of light focused on the area you are searching in.

Well, that is like life. Having made it this far, you understand that merely passing through life is no way to achieve your goals, dreams, and aspirations. If you want to be successful, you will need to harness your energy and focus in a single direction.

Tony Robbins says, "Energy flows where attention goes." To get what you want in life, you must have a clear goal that has purpose and meaning behind it. Once you have that in place, you can focus your energy on your target and become obsessive about it. When you learn how to channel your energy, amazing things happen.

But the same is true for what you don't want. If you focus your attention on the negative or the things you fear, that's exactly what you'll attract. Keep your focus positive and intentional, and you'll be amazed at the results.

What happens when you get off track?

As mentioned earlier, one of the best analogies for your journey in life is GPS. You put in your origin and your destination and start moving. Sometimes, though, you take a wrong turn. The GPS doesn't say, "You're screwed, sorry. You're not going to get there." It simply recalibrates and guides you back on track.

Just like when you're driving and miss a turn, life can get off track— but that doesn't mean it's over. If your goal was to become a corporate CEO and things didn't go as planned, it's okay. You can recalibrate and find a new route to the same destination.

You have a purpose, and no matter how many wrong turns you take, you can still get there. Yes, there may be consequences for those detours, and it might take more time or energy, but if you stay focused on your goal, you'll eventually reach it.

When you understand that a missed step or a wrong turn isn't disastrous, it frees you to make different decisions. You might become bolder, taking shortcuts that can get you there a little faster. It's like driving through town when all the lights are synchronized to be green—you're in the flow, and everything just works.

Remember, it's not about avoiding mistakes; it's about how you respond to them and keep moving forward toward your destination.

How to Focus on What Matters

- **Find Quiet Time:** Busy doesn't always mean productive. Block out quiet time to reflect on what's essential. This clarity helps you prioritize your goals. Whether it's watching a sunrise or sitting in stillness, quiet moments allow you to sort through what truly matters.

- **Remember Your Why:** Keep your purpose front and center. Regularly remind yourself of why you're doing what you do. Ask how you can reduce time spent on distractions and focus more on what you love. Gradual shifts lead to big results.

- **Use a Vision Board or Planner:** Visual cues like a vision board or planner help you stay connected to your long-term goals. Write down your ideas and tasks, then filter them to see which align with your vision. This clarity helps you stay focused and discard distractions.

- **Align Activities with Your Goals:** Define your goals and ensure your daily tasks align with them. Each morning, visualize your day and block out time for important tasks. At day's end, reflect on whether you moved closer to your goals, and adjust your actions for the next day.

- **Set Micro-Goals:** Break your long-term goals into daily micro-goals. Choose up to four critical tasks to complete each day. Whether they are work-related, personal, or household tasks, focusing on just a few priorities ensures steady progress.

- **Plan for the Long Term:** Life is a marathon, not a sprint. Set goals for different timeframes (one month, six months, one year, etc.) and outline the steps needed to achieve them. Keeping your long-term vision in sight helps prevent short-term distractions from derailing your progress.

- **Schedule Weekly Check-Ins:** Regularly review your goals and progress. Weekly check-ins keep you accountable and help you adjust when distractions arise. This habit ensures you stay on track.

- **Focus on Quality Over Quantity:** Quality work requires focus. Plan your tasks and give them your full attention. Avoid multitasking and dedicate time to doing each task well. Focusing on quality ensures that your work stands out.

By incorporating these practical steps into your daily life, you can enhance your ability to focus on what truly matters and make consistent progress toward your goals.

Step 7 - Givers Gain

"Give, and it will be given to you. A good measure, pressed down, shaken together, and running over will be poured into your lap. For with the measure you use, it will be measured to you." ~**Luke 6:38 NIV**

"No one has ever become poor by giving." -~**Anne Frank**

I remember when I was a newlywed, and I would do the dishes after dinner. I am ashamed now to admit it, but I did not do the dishes because it was helpful to my wife. No. I did the dishes because I read somewhere that sex began in the kitchen. I thought the premise of the book was that if a husband wanted more sex in his marriage, all he had to do was help a little in the kitchen. Unfortunately, I missed the author's point. I have since reread the book and now understand what he was trying to get at in his book.

You see, I was giving to get. Not out of unselfish love for my wife. No, I was trying to play the game. What happened was that after several weeks of doing the dishes and not getting the result I wanted, I began to resent my wife for not noticing my gift and not giving me one in return.

Colossians 3:23 in the Bible says, "Whatever you do, work at it with all your heart, as working for the Lord, not for human masters."

Once I came to realize that being helpful in the kitchen was an opportunity to show my wife how much I loved her, the resentment I felt went away. I was no longer giving her a gift to get something in return. I was simply honoring her through an act of service. I was working for God.

Givers Gain is a philosophy based on the law of reciprocity.

It is one of life's many paradoxes that we limit the power of our giving by always expecting something in return. What we do not realize is that if we can learn to give without any thought or desire to get something back, we multiply our return on what we give. Think about the things you do for others, and how often do you expect to get something back? There is an unwritten or expressed expectation that the recipient is bound to give back when we need it.

It has been discovered that the expectations we feel when "giving to get" causes more stress than joy. They destroy the entire purpose of giving. The expectations eventually lead to disappointment and resentment. This disappointment is often the root cause of issues in our relationships.

So, how do you begin to shift your mindset about giving? Before doing something for another person, ask yourself, "What is my expectation?" The most acceptable answer, as cheesy as it may sound, is "To feel good and show love." That is it. You cannot control how others accept or repay your kindness, but you can manage your expectations about the gift. When the intention is simply to feel good and show love, it completely changes the dynamic of the gift.

The Side Effects of Generosity

- **Giving Makes You Happy:** A 2008 study by Harvard Business School Professor Michael Norton found that giving money to others lifted the giver's happiness more than spending it on themselves. When you give, it activates parts of the brain associated with pleasure, social connection, and trust, creating a "warm glow" effect. Scientists believe that endorphins in the brain are released by altruistic behavior, producing a positive feeling known as the "helper's high."

- **Giving Keeps You Healthy:** Giving helps others, but it also benefits the giver. Studies show that giving can boost physical and mental health, lower blood pressure, increase self-esteem, and reduce stress levels.

- **Giving Promotes Social Connection:** When you give to others, your generosity is often reciprocated. It might not come back from the same person, but it often comes back in some form. Positive social interactions are crucial for good mental and physical health. As researcher John Cacioppo noted, "The more extensive the reciprocal altruism born of social connection, the greater the advance toward health, wealth, and happiness."

- **Giving Enhances Life's Satisfaction:** When you give to others, you feel more satisfied with your own life. Givers tend to cope better with life's challenges, possibly because they gain perspective by helping those less fortunate. Giving brings meaning to your life and makes it worthwhile, helping you avoid dwelling on your problems.

- **Giving Spreads Joy:** Giving spreads joy to others in ways you may not even realize. When you bring joy to others, you also experience joy in return. You create connections that you might not have had otherwise, making the world a happier place, one act of kindness at a time.

- **Giving Teaches Responsibility:** Giving often involves making sacrifices. Some people donate regardless of their financial standing. Learning to sacrifice teaches responsibility, helps you manage your spending habits, and shows you that you don't need much to be happy. Sometimes, less is more.

- **Giving Cultivates Self-Worth:** Whether for selfless or selfish reasons, giving brings a sense of self-worth. The joy of helping others boosts your self-esteem. There's nothing wrong with feeling proud of your generosity and using that feeling to inspire further acts of kindness.

- **Giving Strengthens Personal Values:** Many people give because they feel it's a moral duty to help others, rooted in their values and principles. Acting on these powerful feelings of responsibility enhances our values and makes us feel like we're living a truly worthwhile life.

I hope I've shown you the power of giving first. Don't wait for someone to show you love—be the one to show love first. Don't wait for respect—start by giving it to others. Set the example. Focus on excelling in your current job instead of chasing another that seems more fulfilling. And in your relationships, don't wait for your friends to invest time and energy—take the initiative and invest in them yourself.

10 Things You Can Give That Cost Little or Nothing

1. **Time**: Spend time with someone who needs company, whether it's a friend, family member, or someone in your community.

2. **Compliments**: Offer genuine compliments to brighten someone's day and boost their confidence.

3. **A Smile**: Smile at people you meet. A simple smile can make a big difference in someone's day.

4. **Kind Words**: Speak words of encouragement and support. A kind word can uplift someone and make them feel valued.

5. **Listening Ear**: Offer to listen to someone who needs to talk. Sometimes, just being there to listen is a great gift.

6. **Acts of Kindness**: Perform small acts of kindness, like holding the door open, helping someone carry their groceries, or letting someone go ahead of you in line.

7. **Knowledge and Advice**: Share your knowledge or offer advice based on your experiences. This can be especially valuable in guiding someone through a difficult situation.

8. **A Helping Hand**: Help someone with tasks or chores, such as gardening, cleaning, or running errands.

9. **Letters or Notes**: Write a heartfelt letter or note to someone expressing your appreciation or sharing a positive message.

10. **Volunteering**: Volunteer your time at local organizations or events. Giving your time to help others can have a profound impact on both you and the people you assist.

These simple gestures can have a significant impact on others and foster a sense of community and connection. By incorporating these simple actions into your daily routine, you'll cultivate a giving attitude that benefits both you and those around you. Remember, it's the small, consistent acts of generosity that create the biggest impact.

Step 8 - You Can't Do It Alone

"Walk with the wise and become wise, for a companion of fools suffers harm."
~ **Provers 13:20 NIV**

"Surround yourself with only people who are going to lift you higher."

~ **Oprah Winfrey**

I can look back through my life and identify people at every stage that allowed me to be successful. In high school, it was a close group of guys who were like brothers. A girlfriend and her family who saw my potential and encouraged me to shift my thinking.

Then in college, it was a roommate who helped me navigate being away from home for the first time and encouraged me to become a campus bus driver. Then it was a close group of friends and study partners who taught me how to be in college. It sounds weird, I know, but as a first-generation college student, I had no idea how to be a college student.

Then it was my wife. We met in college, and she was the one who taught me how to study and provided me with my "Why" for college. Up until that point, I didn't have a reason other than it beat being at home, and someone had expected me to go to college. But I didn't have a plan beyond college. I had never really thought about it. When I met Kimbra, that all changed. She began to ask questions and quiz me on what my future plans included. She forced me to take college seriously and to study. You can look at my college transcript and see the semester Kimbra and I met. I never made anything less than a B after I met Kimbra. Before I met her, I had never made anything better than a C. Funny how much of a difference reading and studying make.

Then it was my wife's family, the Willmons. We moved to West Texas, and it was through her family that I began my professional career. Being married to a Willmon made a difference. I was forever known as "that boy who married a Willmon girl" or that "kid married to Ike's granddaughter." When it came time for me to pivot careers and begin a life of public service, my success came from my boss, Rick Osburn, who for the life of me, I don't know why he hired me or invested so much time in me. He saw something I didn't, and if not for this constant pruning and nurturing, I would not be writing these words today. We accomplished a lot in Levelland, and it was due to a lot of people working together to make it happen.

Now, as my career has continued to blossom, I have been blessed every step of the way with people willing to help. Some friends, some mentors, some colleagues. The trick is to recognize that you have the power to choose your circle.

Early on in my career as an economic developer, I received some advice from my mentor, Buzz David, who said I could choose the party crowd or the professional crowd. It was my choice, but I had better choose wisely because my future depended on it. I am grateful he took the time to explain just how much was riding on the people I decided to surround myself with.

I never want to be the smartest person in the room, and I don't need to be the fastest or the strongest either. You only get better by surrounding yourself with people who are better than you. If you're always winning, you're not growing—there's no challenge pushing you to improve. Growth comes from failure and striving to be better, which only happens when you step into uncomfortable situations. You need people in your life who will call you out and say, "That's a dumb idea—you need to change it." I know that can feel painful, but without that process, I wouldn't be where I am today.

Have you ever seen an award acceptance speech where the recipients did not offer appreciation to those who helped them get to where they are? Whether it is a business legend, an athlete, a musician, or an actor, successful people know the importance of surrounding themselves with the right people. They know they cannot achieve success all alone. Regardless of all your hard work, good luck, and skills, success most often depends on the people you decide to make a part of your journey.

As you start networking, pay attention and seek out smart people from whom you can learn. It is essential to gain new perspectives. Engaging with intelligent individuals can eliminate blind spots and open your eyes to things you never knew existed. Your circle of influence can help you raise your expectations for yourself. They spark interest in you and introduce you to new concepts, ideas, and opportunities.

Are you asking yourself, "How do I know who I should hang out with or if they are good for me?" Good. That is how you start. It starts by asking questions. Is this person someone I admire? Are they someone I want to model? Do their actions match their words? Get used to continually evaluating your relationships. Is being around this person moving me closer to my desired life or not. You only have so many hours in the day and so many days in your life. Don't waste time with people moving you away from your goal. Get really good at pruning your social tree.

How to Build Your Dream Team

- **Connect with People You Admire:** Follow people you respect, even if it's just online. Engage with their posts, ask questions, and join conversations. Meaningful connections can start this way.

- **Take Online Connections Offline:** After building a rapport online, invite them out for coffee or a meal. Meeting in person fosters deeper connections and the chance to share ideas face-to-face.

- **Volunteer:** Join volunteer efforts to meet generous, like-minded individuals. Giving your time to good causes often brings you into circles of smart, compassionate people.

- **Attend Events Where Smart People Gather:** Go to places like museums, seminars, and conferences where intellectually curious people gather. Engage in meaningful conversations and exchange ideas.

- **Leverage Your Network:** Ask friends or colleagues to introduce you to their circles. They can connect you with events and gatherings where you can meet more people who inspire growth.

- **Step Outside Your Comfort Zone:** Be open to differing viewpoints. Listen and learn from people with perspectives that challenge you. Growth happens when you're willing to step beyond the familiar.

- **Engage with Everyone, Avoid Assumptions:** Don't judge people too quickly—everyone has something to offer. Listen more than you speak, and stay open to learning from everyone, no matter their background.

By following these steps, you can build a network of smart, inspiring individuals who will help you grow and achieve your goals.

Step 9 - Shift to a Positive Mindset

"Finally, brothers, whatever is true, whatever is honorable, whatever is just, whatever is pure, whatever is lovely, whatever is commendable, if there is any excellence, if there is anything worthy of praise, think about these things."
~Philippians 4:8 NIV

"Positive thinking won't allow you to do anything, but it will allow you to do everything better than negative thinking will." ~Zig Ziglar

As part of our summer fun, we enjoy activities on the lake. The kids love knee boarding and wake surfing around the little cove where we stay. When they first started, they only wanted to go in the morning when the water was beautiful and calm, and there were very few waves.

However, they soon realized that just going round and round in calm water wasn't all that fun. The kids rapidly grew bored with the lack of challenge. So, we began venturing out later in the afternoon when there were a lot of other boats out on the water, creating tons of waves.

Now, riding these waves was difficult at first, and often they might even let go if they thought a particular set of waves looked too big for them to handle. I would circle back around and ask why they let go, and they would chastise me for not warning them about the waves we were about to hit.

But slowly, they began to brave the oncoming waves, and each time they made it through, it gave them the confidence to face the next set. They learned a valuable lesson out there on the water. They discovered that if they wanted to have fun, waves were just part of the deal.

Rarely in life do we get calm waters in which to operate. Accept waves are coming and see them as a way to improve. Know that you're going to faceplant from time to time, but failure is not fatal as long as you dare to ride again.

Each time out, you'll build your confidence to handle future challenges, and this will lead to success.

Maintaining a positive mindset is one part of practicing what Guy Winch, Ph.D., a licensed psychologist, keynote speaker, and author of Emotional First Aid, refers to as Emotional Hygiene.

The actual process of being mindful of our psychological health and adopting brief daily habits to monitor and address psychological wounds when we sustain them.

Just like we wash every day, put on deodorant, and brush our teeth, it's important to practice emotional hygiene. There are things we experience every day that can cause us to have what Zig Ziglar used to call "Stinkin' Thinkin'."

Practicing emotional hygiene allows us to clean up this negative thinking and help keep our attitudes in check. It's essential to build a practice of having a positive mindset where you see problems as potential learning processes rather than just another hill to climb.

Now, let's talk more about how to develop a positive mindset. It's important to know that being positive doesn't necessarily mean merely smiling and looking happy all the time. It's more of a life view and choosing to concentrate on everything in life that's good.

Generally, it is much easier to be pessimistic than to be optimistic. People will often look at something as half-empty glass instead of half-full glass; they'd rather criticize and complain than express appreciation for everything that happens. To live a life worth living, you must take intentional actions to develop a healthy and positive mindset. With practice, you'll find that being positive is not only easier but also far more impactful than being negative.

What is a positive mindset?

You likely already have an idea of what a positive mindset is, but starting with a definition is always useful. An excellent overall description is this definition from Remez Sasson, author, blogger, and founder of the Success Consciousness website (n.d.):

"Positive thinking is a mental and emotional mindset that focuses on the bright side of life and expects positive results."

I like to think of a positive mindset as approaching life's challenges with a positive outlook. It does not necessarily mean avoiding or ignoring the bad things. Instead, it involves making the most of the potentially negative situations, seeing the best in other people, and viewing myself and my abilities in a positive light.

Having a positive mindset implies making a habit of positive thinking, continuously looking for a silver lining, and making the best out of any scenario you find yourself experiencing.

Characteristics and Traits of a Positive Mindset

There are many characteristics and traits connected with positive thinking, including:

- **Optimism:** This trait helps you stay hopeful and find the good in any situation. Optimism can boost your overall happiness, improve your mental health, and increase your ability to handle stress.

- **Acceptance:** Accepting that things won't always go your way allows you to learn from mistakes and move forward. This helps you adapt to changes, reduce frustration, and maintain a balanced perspective.

- **Resilience:** Bouncing back from adversity, deception, and failure keeps you moving forward despite challenges. Resilience builds your strength, enhances your problem-solving skills, and helps you achieve long-term goals.

- **Gratitude:** Actively appreciating the beautiful aspects of your life promotes a sense of contentment and joy. Gratitude improves your emotional well-being, strengthens relationships, and increases your overall life satisfaction.

- **Consciousness/Mindfulness:** Focusing your mind on conscious understanding and positive things enhances your awareness and concentration. Mindfulness reduces stress, improves emotional regulation, and fosters a deeper connection with the present moment.

- **Integrity:** Embracing honesty, fairness, and simplicity builds trust and respect in your relationships. Integrity ensures that your actions align with your values, leading to a more fulfilling and authentic life.

These traits not only help build a positive mindset but also enhance many other aspects of your life. By cultivating optimism, acceptance, resilience, gratitude, mindfulness, and integrity, you can improve your mental and emotional well-being, strengthen your relationships, and achieve greater personal and professional success.

Why is a positive mindset considered the key to success?

What is it about having a positive mindset that's so important, so powerful, and so life-changing? The features and characteristics of a positive mindset offer us some insight. You'll see several advantages connected to optimism, resilience, and gratitude.

If you look through the literature, you'll find that awareness and integrity lead to an improved quality of life, while acceptance and gratitude can elevate you from living a "good life" to a "great life."

But don't worry—this isn't about being positive all the time. I'm not suggesting that just "thinking happy thoughts" will magically bring you all the success you want in life, and I certainly don't believe that optimism is the answer to every situation, every minute of the day.

A positive mindset isn't about ignoring the negative or pretending everything is always perfect. It's about taking both the positive and negative into account and remaining generally optimistic. This balanced approach helps you stay resilient in the face of challenges, open to new opportunities, and motivated to keep moving forward.

In essence, a positive mindset equips you with the mental tools to handle life's ups and downs more effectively, ultimately leading you to greater success.

How to Cultivate a Positive Mindset

- **Start Your Day with Positive Affirmations:** How you begin your day sets up how the rest of the day will unfold. Are there times when you've woken up late in a panic, spilled coffee while rushing to work, and then felt like nothing good happened for the rest of the day? This is because you started the day with a negative emotion. You must start your day with positive affirmations. Even if you wake up late, you should still stop for a moment to say, "Today will be a great day," or "Something good is going to come out of today." You can even do these things on your commute. You'll be surprised how much your day will improve.

- **Stay Focused on What You Want:** You can't achieve success without knowing what that is to you. Remember your purpose, vision, goals, and mini goals. What are your plans for the day? Connecting your tasks to your desired outcome will improve your mood.

- **Let Go of Your Need for Perfection:** Trying to do every single thing perfectly will only lead to stress and frustration, because it is impossible to be perfect in everything you do. Strive for progress and excellence. Perfection leaves no room for improvement, and what fun is that?

- **Appreciate the Little Things:** It is inevitable that some days won't feel so great. You are going to encounter obstacles. When you do, focus on the benefits, no matter how little or unimportant it is. For example, if you get stuck in traffic, instead of feeling frustrated about a situation you cannot change, think instead about how you have more time to listen to your favorite podcast or songs. If the supermarket is out of an ingredient for the meal you planned, think how exciting it will be to try something new.

- **Find Humor in Bad Situations:** In trying situations, allow yourself to find humor. Remind yourself that the situation will probably make for a good story later, and try to make it light by cracking a joke about it (even if only internally when situations require tact). Let's say you were laid off. Yes, the situation may be hard, and you'll feel sad and frustrated. But for a moment, allow yourself to imagine the most ridiculous job you could pursue next, like being a rat trainer or candy sculptor. Enjoy a moment to laugh and then get to work on your next opportunity with a better attitude.

- **Turn Failures into Lessons:** You are going to make a lot of mistakes and experience failure multiple times. Everyone does. Instead of focusing on how you failed and beating yourself up about it, think about what you're going to do to make things right next time. That turns your failure into a lesson. Make sure you learn the lesson and don't make the same mistakes again.

- **Transform Negative Self-Talk into Positive Self-Talk:** Negative self-talk tends to creep up without being noticed. You may start to think how bad you are at something or why you shouldn't have attempted a particular thing. Dwelling on these kinds of thoughts can turn into internalized beliefs that limit your potential. The moment you become aware of negative self-talk, pause and replace the thought with a positive one. For instance, when you think you are bad at something, stop and envision yourself being really great at it. Then, note the steps you need to take in order to fulfill that vision.

- **Consider When You've Seen Positive Mindsets in Action:** Identify instances when you've seen people put their positive mindsets to work for them and consider situations in your own life where you can do the same. When was the last time you observed someone look in the eyes of a problem and laugh? Accept what they got without throwing a tantrum? Take an unexpected outcome as an opportunity for fun? Motivate the people around them with positive words? Reverse the tone of a situation with a smile? Show friendliness to complete strangers?

By incorporating these steps into your daily routine, you can cultivate a positive mindset that will enhance your overall well-being and help you tackle life's challenges with optimism and resilience.

Step 10 - Take Massive Action

"Little children let us not love in word or talk but indeed and in truth." 1
~John 3:18 NIV

"The path to success is to take massive, determined action." ~**Tony Robbins**

"83-Year-Old Man Who Walked Miles to Mow His Customers' Lawns Is Surprised with New Truck," read the headline. I was intrigued. It turns out the story was about John Joyce, an 83-year-old Florida resident. He spent months walking several miles a day to his customers' homes. He was their lawn man.

Months earlier, John's transmission went out in his pickup truck, and he didn't have the money to replace it. So, he did what he had to do to get the job done. He walked. The story goes on to explain how a longtime customer, Robert Norton, and his wife, Nikki Norton, created a GoFundMe account, hoping to help Joyce.

As I finished the article, I began to read the comments. I was struck by how all the comments talked about the generosity of those who made the donations. While it is incredible that strangers would rally and help someone in need in such a way, I think the most important lesson was missed.

The thing to remember is John's incredible work ethic, which inspired the donations. An 83-year-old man who was still mowing lawns despite losing his mode of transportation. He never stopped. He didn't sit on the side of the street, begging for a handout. He didn't create excuses for not being able to get the job done. He didn't complain about having to push his mower for miles just to mow a yard. He was working!

How many people today would continue to work if faced with having to push their lawnmower to and from work?

Mr. Joyce is a hero. A guy who didn't whine about the circumstances he was facing or blame others for his luck. No, he kept his head down and continued to grind. John worked! Did you catch that? He worked!

Achieving your goals or succeeding in any field of endeavor requires action. Not just any action, it demands massive action. Massive Action is the kind of action that most people are unwilling to take to achieve success. If you are not willing to go the extra mile to accomplish your goal, then that just means it was not that important of a goal for you.

When I speak to audiences, one of the points I make is the importance of the law of sowing and reaping. If you want to reap a harvest, then you need to plant. And if you need to plant, the best way to get started is to start digging.

You don't stand around and whine about needing help or complain about how hard it is to plant all the seeds. You grab a shovel and start planting. You plant when no one is looking. You plant when people are making fun of you for trying to do it yourself. You plant even when you don't feel like it. And while you're planting, you don't gripe or complain about doing it alone. You plant with a smile because you know something they don't: You know that the effort you put in now will bear fruit in the future. You understand that persistence and dedication lead to success, even if others can't see it yet. While they're busy doubting, you're busy building something meaningful and lasting.

When you do this, something magical happens. It's called momentum. Action creates energy, and that energy turns into momentum, and momentum draws a crowd. Suddenly, people start looking for shovels to help you. Row by row, the seeds get planted, and then the garden gets planted. You accomplish your goal. But it all begins with Y.O.U. picking up the shovel.

If you want your community or your county or your state or our country to be great, inspire those around you to pick up a shovel by picking one up yourself. Start planting the seeds of your desired future now.

Stop whining about how others are not helping create the world you want for yourself. Grab a shovel and start digging! Even if you are 83 years old!

What does it mean to take massive action?

Taking massive action means doing more than the average person would do under particular circumstances. It means going further, breaking boundaries, and reaching for the unexpected.

Taking massive action means having a goal and making the accomplishment of that goal, your duty, obligation, and responsibility. It means taking full ownership and responsibility for your situation.

By taking massive action, you will expand your experience, knowledge, understanding, and opportunities. Taking massive action will naturally bring you more opportunities. You begin to get luckier with opportunities because you are putting yourself out there persistently. When you put yourself out on the line, you will be rewarded.

The idea of taking massive action boils down to two main factors. The first factor comes from your ability to dream and think big about your goals and the objectives you would like to achieve.

Thinking big is something that a lot of people do. However, you won't get very far if all you do is think big because thinking big isn't all it takes. There is a second piece of the puzzle, and that is action. Achieving your goals or succeeding in any field requires action.

How to Create Massive Action in Your Life

- **Clarify Your Desired Objective**: Failure to act often stems from a lack of clarity about your goals. Many people have an idea of what they want to achieve, but their goals are not concrete. A dream is hazy and unclear, making it seem unattainable. Give your dream some clarity to turn it into a concrete goal that inspires action.

  Ask yourself the following questions:

  a. What is it that I want to achieve?

  b. What steps do I need to take to bring this goal to reality?

  c. What exactly do I need to do?

  d. What specific actions will I take?

  e. How will I take these actions? When? Where? For how long?

    f. When do I plan to accomplish this goal? What's my deadline?

Answering these questions will provide you with the clarity you need to achieve your goals.

- **Make Peace with What's to Come**: Gaining clarity about your goal is not enough. You must also be willing to take the massive action required to bring it to reality. People often hold back due to comfort, fear, and uncertainty. To move forward, you must make peace with these feelings and take action anyway.

Acknowledge the following:

    a. What you must do may feel uncomfortable. Be at peace with discomfort.

    b. Fear will try to hold you back. Use fear as fuel to keep moving forward.

    c. Taking massive action will cure your fears.

    d. Embrace uncertainty wholeheartedly. Turn discomfort into a challenge, fear into excitement, and uncertainty into curiosity.

By making peace with what's to come, you can break through the mental barriers holding you back.

- **Make a Wholehearted Commitment**: To accomplish your goals, you need unwavering commitment. Be wholeheartedly dedicated to taking action. Lack of commitment leads to frustration and distraction. Stay focused on your goals, and don't let setbacks deter you.

- **Gain Leverage**: Lack of leverage often stops people from taking massive action. Leverage creates motivation. There are two types of leverage: pain and pleasure.

Ask yourself these questions:

  a. If I take massive action toward my goal, what do I stand to gain?

  b. How will not achieving this goal hurt me? What regrets will I have?

Use these questions to gain the leverage needed to stay motivated and persistent.

- **Think About the Price of Success**: Every goal comes with a cost. Achieving your goals requires sacrifices, such as time, energy, and money. Consider how these sacrifices will affect other areas of your life. Your priorities, commitments, and responsibilities will change as you pursue your goals.

Ask yourself these critical questions:

a. In relation to this goal, what are my top priorities?

b. What do I need to sacrifice to achieve this goal?

c. How do I keep myself focused and motivated during the journey?

Understanding the price of success will prepare you for the commitment required to reach your goals.

- **Create a Sense of Urgency**: Develop an inner drive and desire to act quickly and get things done. A sense of urgency motivates you to push ahead and keep going. It makes you more sensitive and aware, helping you develop brilliant ideas and insights that propel you forward.

By following these steps, you can create massive action in your life and move closer to achieving your goals. Stay committed, embrace discomfort, and maintain a sense of urgency to keep yourself on track.

Step 11 - Always Do the Right Thing

"And let us not grow weary of doing good, for in due season we will reap, if we do not give up." ~**Galatians 6:9 NIV**

"Do what is right, not what is easy nor what is popular." ~Roy T. Bennett

One hot summer afternoon, my friends and I decided to sneak into a private hay meadow to swim and fish in a secluded pond. We'd been told before the field was off limits by the owner and that if he caught us using his pond, he'd call the cops. But the thrill of sneaking into the field and the allure of fishing this hidden spot were just too tempting.

We climbed the fence and made our way to the pond, laughing as we enjoyed the cool water and the freedom of the moment. Everything was perfect until we saw the deputy making his way across the field from the highway.

"Run!" someone shouted, and panic set in. We all scrambled out of the water, grabbing our clothes and fishing gear. Adrenaline pumping, we sprinted toward the fence. Everyone taking off in different directions, making our way to the fence line, trying to avoid getting caught.

I was almost over the fence when I glanced back and saw one of my cousins struggling to help a friend who had twisted her ankle. They were lagging behind, and the sheriff's deputy was getting closer. At that moment, I knew I had a choice to make. Leave 'em behind or go back.

Without a second thought, I turned around and ran back to help them. "Stop right there!" the deputy called out. We froze, knowing we were caught. He approached us with a stern look on his face. "What do you think you're doing here?" he asked.

I took a deep breath and stepped forward. "Sorry, sir. We were just doing a little fishing."

The sheriff looked at the three of us, his expression softening slightly. "You kids know you shouldn't be here. It's trespassing."

"Yes, sir," I replied. "Don't worry, we'll head out and won't come back."

The sheriff nodded, seeing the sincerity in my eyes. "Alright, I'll let you off with a warning this time. But if I catch you here again, there will be consequences. Now get out of here and take care of your friend."

We helped our friend over the fence, and the three of us walked back to the house together. As we walked, my cousin turned to me and said, "Thanks for coming back, bud. You didn't have to do that."

I shrugged, a small smile on my face. "It was the right thing to do. We got into this together, and I wasn't going to leave you to face it alone."

That afternoon, I learned a valuable lesson about doing the right thing. Even when it's hard, even when it means facing trouble, doing what's right makes you feel good about yourself and strengthens your bonds with others. It was a lesson I carried with me into adulthood, shaping the person I am today.

Life isn't about avoiding mistakes or staying out of trouble. It's about owning your mistakes. Standing by the people who matter. Doing the right thing, no matter the cost. In the end, that's what truly makes a difference.

Deep down, we all know right from wrong. The ability to make good choices comes from within. When you consistently choose to do the right thing, the positive results become clear, and that clarity fuels your willpower to keep making the right decisions.

Doing the right thing is how you become the person you want to be and live a life worth living. While it sounds simple, it's one of the hardest things to do. And sometimes, what feels right might not always be the best decision for you.

What exactly is doing the right thing?

Doing the "right" thing means staying true to your values and making choices that align with who you want to be. It's about acting with integrity, even when it's hard or no one's watching. It's taking responsibility for your actions and understanding how they impact others. It's about being compassionate, making sure you're not just looking out for yourself but also lifting up those around you.

At the end of the day, doing the right thing often means making tough decisions—sacrificing convenience for what's right, stepping up when others won't, and keeping your word no matter what. It's not always easy, but it's the foundation of building a life that matters.

Why does doing the right thing matter?

When you consistently do the right thing, good things often come back to you. You tend to get what you give. By adding value and helping others, you'll find that many people want to return the favor—sometimes in ways you didn't expect. Not everyone will, but enough will to make it worthwhile.

Plus, doing the right thing boosts your self-esteem. When you make the right choices, you feel better about yourself. You build confidence and a strong sense of self. But when you choose the wrong path, it chips away at that confidence, leaving you feeling frustrated and empty.

Doing the right thing reinforces that you're worthy of success, and it helps you avoid the trap of self-sabotage. When you know you're making the right choices, you stay on track toward your goals without letting doubt or bad habits derail you.

How to Cultivate the Habit of Doing the Right Thing

- **Start Small:** Doing the right thing doesn't mean you have to move mountains right away. It starts with the small stuff—being honest, keeping your word, and showing up on time. These little choices build momentum. Before you know it, doing the right thing becomes second nature.

- **Trust Your Gut:** You've got that voice inside that usually knows what's right—it's your gut. Don't ignore it. The more you listen to it and act on it, the stronger it gets. Soon enough, doing the right thing will feel like a reflex.

- **Reflect on Your Day:** Every night, take a moment to ask yourself: *Did I show up as the person I want to be?* It's not about perfection; it's about progress. When you reflect on your actions, you reinforce the habit of making the right choices.

- **Surround Yourself with the Right People:** Who you spend time with matters. Surround yourself with people who push you to do better, who call you out when you're slipping, and who lead by example. It's a lot easier to stay on track when your circle holds you accountable.

- **Own Your Mistakes:** Look, nobody gets it right every time. When you mess up—and you will—own it. Don't make excuses; just fix it and move on. The faster you take responsibility, the quicker you get back to doing the right thing.

- **Think Long-Term:** Doing the right thing doesn't always feel great in the moment. Sometimes it's tough. But remember, the real rewards come down the road. Keep your eyes on the bigger picture—your future self will thank you for it.

- **Be Consistent:** You don't need to be perfect, just consistent. Show up every day and make the best choices you can. Over time, those small decisions add up and turn into habits that stick.

Building the habit of doing the right thing isn't about being perfect—it's about making small, consistent choices that align with who you want to be. Keep at it, and it'll become a part of who you are.

By incorporating these practices into your daily life, you can cultivate a habit of doing the right thing, leading to greater self-esteem, success, and overall well-being.

Step 12 - Be A Lifelong Learner

"The fear of the Lord is the beginning of knowledge; fools despise wisdom and instruction." ~**Proverbs 1:7 NIV**

"Live as if you were to die tomorrow. Learn as if you were to live forever." - ~**Mahatma Gandhi**

The first person I knew to be a lifelong learner was my dad. Funny enough, he never finished the eighth grade. He was the oldest of four children, and when he was just ten years old, his mom left. To help make ends meet, he was forced to leave school and start working.

But just because he wasn't in school didn't mean he stopped learning. Over the next sixty years, he became a master plumber, a master electrician, a certified diesel mechanic, a certified welder, a licensed heavy equipment operator, a commercial truck driver, a ham radio operator, and he learned to read and speak Spanish as a second language.

He never stopped learning. He was always curious and consumed information like it was candy. He loved to understand how things worked and usually wanted to master them once he figured it out.

Looking back now, I can see just how lucky I was to have grown up with him as a role model. I must confess that at the time, I hated learning those skills. All I could see was the 5 a.m. wake-up calls and the hours of blood, sweat, and tears that usually followed. Now, I can genuinely appreciate the education I received while working alongside him all those years. The other thing I appreciate is the habit of learning he instilled in me. I may have spent my years since learning a different set of skills, but I remain a lifelong learner.

One thing highly successful people have in common is the belief in being lifelong learners. No matter how much they achieve, they keep learning and growing. Adopting this mindset opens countless doors. Every day you commit to learning, growing, and developing yourself, you add value to who you are and what you offer to the world. The rewards? Greater knowledge, improved skills, and increased income. In today's ever-changing world, becoming a lifelong learner is essential to achieving and maintaining success.

When we think of learning, we often picture formal education—school, college, or university. While formal education and qualifications are important for many careers, learning isn't confined to the classroom. In fact, formal education can help you maximize your potential, find more satisfying work, and achieve greater success in your career. But that's just one type of learning.

There are countless ways to grow your knowledge and skills outside formal education. Life constantly presents opportunities to learn— so why not make it intentional? Embrace every moment as a chance to grow and develop yourself. With today's technology, there's no shortage of ways to learn something new or master a skill. To succeed in this fast-paced world, you need to adopt the mindset of constant learning. And remember, learning can be a joyous adventure, not just a necessity.

Lifelong learning is about maintaining a positive, proactive attitude toward acquiring knowledge. It boosts confidence, enhances self-esteem, and makes us more adaptable when changes come our way. Learning doesn't just challenge our ideas—it enriches our lives and makes them more fulfilling. And yes, it can even be fun.

Learning is intentional and driven by choice for lifelong learners. This ongoing process deepens your understanding of the world, provides fresh insights, and improves your perspective, helping you create a more joyful and meaningful life.

People often pursue lifelong learning for two main reasons— personal and professional development, and usually both. What's surprising is how much personal growth can enhance your career and how professional growth can enrich your personal life. Studies show continuous learning can delay or prevent certain illnesses, like dementia. Staying mentally engaged keeps your mind sharp and leads to a more satisfying life at any age. The benefits of lifelong learning are not just theoretical. They are real and tangible, waiting for you to seize them.

Personal development takes many forms. You might want to expand your knowledge in a hobby you love or learn something new that enhances your life, like pottery, business management, or even ancestral research. You might be preparing for a trip and want to explore the culture, history, and language of your destination. Or you've discovered a passion for a new field and decided to pursue a degree later in life. The world is full of opportunities for learning, and the more open-minded you are, the more you can discover and grow.

On the professional side, learning new skills and knowledge enhances your work performance and increases your earning potential. Doctors, lawyers, teachers, and professionals across countless industries engage in continuous learning to stay at the top of their fields. While professional development often includes formal activities like seminars, conferences, or workshops, it can also happen informally—through discussions with colleagues, personal research, or learning from peers.

There are endless reasons to pursue learning throughout your life. It can help you become a top performer, increase promotions and financial growth opportunities, and deepen your understanding of the world around you. Lifelong learning is the key to unlocking your potential and living a more successful, fulfilling life.

How To Become a Lifelong Learner

- **Make and Maintain a List of What You Want to Learn:** This is an excellent way to start. Make notes of what you want to learn, then prioritize which topics you'll investigate first. Then, list books, articles, and papers you want to read for each. You can update this list with new materials as you discover them.

- **Read More and More Frequently:** Subscribe to digital magazines, blogs, and newsletters on topics that interest you. Use apps like Pinterest, Pocket, and Flipboard to curate articles from around the web. For deeper dives, explore podcasts, audiobooks, and e-books on platforms like Audible or Kindle. For academic content, tools like Google Scholar, Medium, or ResearchGate are your go-tos. Stay curious. With so much information available at your fingertips, you can learn anywhere, anytime. And remember, reading is still one of the best ways to broaden your understanding and keep growing.

- **Interact with Intelligent People:** Go to that network I covered in "Step 8 - Surround Yourself with Smart People," and check in with your contacts. Talk to influencers and organize meetings on social channels to explore ideas. Keep in touch with those who inspire you to learn about your journey.

- **Be a Teacher:** You don't need to join the teaching profession to help people learn. You can become a mentor, give a presentation to peers, or share knowledge with business prospects. Sharing knowledge by teaching others what you know is not only a gift but also a test of your understanding. Encourage your "students" to launch projects and teach them what you now know about planning them with purpose, vision, and goals.

- **Explore New Ways of Learning:** There are so many new resources and ways to learn, and exploring them can be an education in itself. Understanding how to learn more effectively is a priceless ability. Using personal learning environments like GoConqr.com, you can use established learning methods to discover fresh learning skills. You can also learn new methods of sharing new information once you've learned it. Drawing diagrams, watching movies, making mind maps, and learning with music are alternative methods of learning and teaching you can explore.

- **Join a Diverse Group of Students:** Find and join online virtual learning groups that bring together individuals with diverse experiences and backgrounds. Insights from a range of sources will enrich your quest for understanding.

- **Take All Opportunities for Work-Related Training:** Most professional roles include a certain level of continuing education, even if it is just opportunities to enroll in employer-sponsored workshops or other training support.

- **Make Learning a Daily Priority:** Stop saying, "One day I'll learn more about . . ." and start today. Whether you're a professor, student, professional, or anyone else, make learning part of your daily routine. Commit to expanding your knowledge now—don't wait for the perfect moment. The time to prioritize your growth is today.

- **Don't Ignore the Curious Side of You:** A curious mind is a receptacle for learning. The secret of being a genius is to carry the wonderment of your childhood into your adulthood. Einstein stated that asking questions and imagination were more important than intelligence. It should be natural for us to be inquisitive and ask questions all of the time, such as "How?" "What?" "When?" "Where?" "Who?" and "Why?" It is through questions that we seek the answers that we need to learn. Develop your power of creativity by developing your curiosity and eagerness to learn new things.

By integrating these habits into your daily routine, you can become a lifelong learner, continuously updating your knowledge and skills for personal and professional growth.

Step 13 - Get Some Grit

*"Blessed is the one who perseveres under trial because, having stood the test, that person will receive the crown of life that the Lord has promised to those who love him." ~**James 1:12 NIV***

*"If you're never able to tolerate a little bit of pain and discomfort, you'll never get better." ~**Angela Duckworth***

It was a hot summer day, and I stood watching as my dad climbed the light tower of the community baseball field with this blow torch to remove some metal from the tower and replace it with brackets for the new lights.

I remember being in awe of my dad as he climbed the tower with one hand while holding the torch in the other. He was in his standard dress, including his long-sleeve starched denim shirt and jeans, with a welder's hat turned backward. He settled into position, lit his torch, and began cutting away the old metal brackets.

That kind of work creates hot molten metal that falls away, and I danced around the bottom of the tower, tending his lines to ensure they didn't tangle as he worked. The challenge was not getting a piece of hot slag down my shirt as it fell from above. Something I was very good at doing, but often at the cost of my dad yelling at me for jerking the lines.

At one point, I remember looking up and seeing his hat catch fire. My dad quickly finished the last cut above his head and then was able to turn off the torch, free his hand, and brush his hat off his head. As he climbed down the tower, I could see the area of his head where a quarter-sized piece of slag had burnt through his hair and into his skull. I asked him if he was okay and why he hadn't stopped when he felt the metal burning his head. His answer: "What and drop the torch or fall off the tower? Not an option. I had to finish." I remember thinking, "What the hell?" And that is where I got my grit.

"If it were easy, everyone would do." Grit is your capacity to remain enthusiastic and persevere at something when you are confronted with barriers. According to the Merriam-Webster dictionary, grit in the context of behavior is defined as "firmness of character; indomitable spirit."

I'm not suggesting that you have to let hot metal burn a hole in your head, but in life, if you want to achieve anything worth achieving, you will have to find the mental toughness to push through when things get tough.

Grit is about endurance. To persevere means to stay with it, to work hard even after having problems or failures. Even when there are no intense feelings or infatuation in the work you are doing, it's all about remaining committed to a job despite it being hard or tedious.

Why Is Grit Important?

Grit is essential because it is a driver of success, regardless of what talent and intellect contribute. Of course, being intelligent and talented is fantastic, but we need the capacity to persevere and prosper. Talent can only be unmet potential without grit. Talent can only be a success with effort. Without effort, talent can only be an unfulfilled potential.

Perseverance is probably one of a person's most admirable characteristics. It's the ability to do or achieve anything, irrespective of setbacks.

"No great achievement is possible without persistent work." Bertrand Russell

Persistence is a distinctive characteristic of those who succeed in life compared to those who do not have it. Many can pursue goals and plans, but few are successful because few keep working on their goals and projects until they achieve success.

Most stop or even leave before the beginning of their journey. Hardness, discomfort, and uncertainty often lead to quitting or giving up. Ordinary people allow their fears and doubts to paralyze them. They lack the motivation necessary to push them through the hard times.

If you want to be extraordinary and alter your life and attain success, you must develop grit. Cultivating the mental toughness needed to meet obstacles head-on and persist anyway.

How to Develop Grit

- **Ask Yourself: What Do I Want?**:

  "If you don't know where you are going, you will probably end up somewhere else." – *Yogi Berra*

  Most people can't tell you what they want, let alone why they want it. Recognize your wants or wishes before you can develop persistence. Start by asking yourself what you want and writing it all down.

- **Find Out What Motivates You**:

  "He who has a why can endure anyhow." – *Friedrich Nietzsche*

  The "why" is the most important question you can ask yourself. Understanding your core motivations helps you pursue your goals with passion and grit. Take your list from the first step and begin asking yourself "why" you want those things.

- **Describe the Next Best Step**:

  Now that you have the what and the why, it's time to break down the how. Identify the next best step you can take to achieve your goals. You don't need every step mapped out, just the next one. After taking that step, repeat the process. Soon, you'll find yourself well on your way to achieving your goals.

- **Maintain a Positive Mindset**:

  Success can be simple, but it isn't easy. Expect to experience defeat and failure along the way. Maintaining a positive mindset helps you develop persistence. Focus on your objectives and avoid negative thinking that can distract you from your goals.

- **Be a Fighter**:

  Adopt the mindset of a fighter. People with a fighting spirit are persistent and don't let circumstances push them around. Remember Rocky Balboa's words: "It ain't about how hard you hit. It's about how hard you can get hit and keep moving forward."

- **Tap into Your Feelings**:

Emotions are powerful when it comes to persistence. Focus on the feeling of achieving your goal. How will it feel when you succeed? Choose your thoughts wisely, as they produce your feelings. Tapping into this truth will help you push through tough times.

- **Find People Who Persevere**:

One of the best ways to develop grit is by modeling others who have it. Look for stories of people who faced challenges and overcame them. Talk to successful individuals and learn about the obstacles they face. You'll see that every success story is filled with hurdles that have to be overcome.

- **Build Your Mastermind Group**:

A mastermind group consists of individuals who can help you achieve your objectives. Surround yourself with positive, like-minded people. Avoid those with pessimistic and cynical attitudes, as they can drain your energy. Remember, you are influenced by the people you meet and the books you read.

- **Make Discipline a Habit**:

Jim Rohm once said, "Discipline is the bridge between goals and accomplishments." Part of having grit is the discipline to keep going even when you don't feel like it. By making discipline a habit, you can bypass emotional obstacles and succeed. The more times you face resistance and push through it, the stronger your grit becomes.

In the end, there's no magic formula for developing grit. Like anything else, you must work to cultivate and improve your ability to meet obstacles and keep going. When you fail, and you will fail, give yourself some grace. But stick to it.

Gratitude

Dear Reader,

As I bring this book to a close, I want to take a moment to express my heartfelt gratitude to you. Thank you for picking up this book, for investing your precious time in reading it, and for seeking to learn and grow. Your dedication to personal development and your willingness to embrace new ideas truly inspire me.

I believe with all my heart that it was no accident you found your way to these pages. In God's grand design, every step we take and every choice we make has a purpose. You were meant to read this book, to absorb its lessons, and to carry its messages forward in your life. You have a unique path laid out before you, and I am honored to have been a part of your journey, even if just for a while.

Now that you've reached the end, I ask you: What will you do with the knowledge you've gained? How will you take these insights and apply them to your life, your work, and your relationships? Remember, knowledge is powerful, but it is action that truly transforms. I encourage you to take bold steps, make courageous decisions, and persist through the challenges you will inevitably face.

Know that you are loved. I see you, your potential, and the incredible value you bring to this world. Each of us has a unique contribution to make, and I believe you are capable of greatness. You have within you the strength, the wisdom, and the grit to overcome any obstacle and achieve your dreams.

As you move forward, keep in mind the importance of being a lifelong learner, of doing the right thing even when it's hard, and of cultivating a positive mindset. Surround yourself with good people, stay curious, and never stop striving for better. Remember that setbacks are just setups for comebacks, and every failure is a lesson in disguise.

In closing, I want to leave you with a blessing: May you always find the courage to follow your heart, the wisdom to discern your path, and the strength to carry on when times get tough. May you be surrounded by love and support, and may you find joy and fulfillment in all that you do.

Thank you once again for allowing me to be a part of your journey. I am grateful for you, and I am cheering you on every step of the way. #FistBump

Make it a great life,

Super Dave Quinn, CEcD

About The Author

Super Dave Quinn, CEcD, is a dynamic business coach, podcast host, sought-after speaker, and certified economic development expert with over 20 years of experience helping communities, businesses, and leaders achieve transformational growth.

As the founder of Day One Experts, Dave specializes in providing actionable strategies for cities, developers, and organizations looking to drive meaningful change and long-term success.

His expertise spans economic development, business leadership, and strategic planning, making him a trusted advisor to both the public and private sectors. Known for his engaging, no-nonsense approach, Super Dave delivers powerful insights that inspire audiences to take bold steps toward their goals.

As a speaker, Super Dave captivates his audience with real-world stories, practical advice, and a deep passion for helping others unlock their potential. Super Dave's message will leave a lasting impact if you're seeking to motivate your team, foster growth in your organization, or build stronger business relationships.

With a proven track record of success and a commitment to helping others overcome obstacles, Super Dave Quinn, CEcD, is the go-to expert for those looking to achieve substantial results in their personal and professional lives.

To book Super Dave Quinn for speaking engagements or consulting services visit SuperDaveQuinn.com or D1Experts.com. Or you can contact him at SuperDave@D1Experts.com

www.ingramcontent.com/pod-product-compliance
Lightning Source LLC
Chambersburg PA
CBHW070755120626
46557CB00002B/606